Thirty, Dirty, and Drowning

A Retrospective on My First Thirty Years of Life

Written during the fifteen days surrounding my thirtieth birthday

K Sastre

Parson's Porch Books

Thirty, Dirty, and Drowning
ISBN: Softcover 978-1-955581-79-0
Copyright © 2022 by K Sastre

Parson's Porch Books is an imprint of Parson's Porch *&* Company (PP*&*C) in Cleveland, Tennessee. PP*&*C is an innovative organization which raises money by publishing books of noted authors, representing all genres. Its face and voice is **David Russell Tullock** (dtullock@parsonsporch.com).

Parson's Porch *&* Company *turns books into bread & milk* by sharing its profits with the poor.

www.parsonsporch.com

Thirty, Dirty, and Drowning

Special thanks to:

Everyone who participated in Just Write It 2020
Kelly Hanwright
Lydia Nascimento
Adri Clement
Marie Headrick
Ilena Holder

The Start

February 1, 2020

Part 1

It all began the typical way
There was darkness and pain
Storms that raged on without ceasing

I was thrust into the ocean
Drifting in the current
Bobbing in the waves

I learned to swim
Tread water to stay alive
But I also tasted drowning

I knew the boats were not for me
That the rafts would come and go
It was never my place to be on dry land
Though I had no love for the sea

Part 2

A child raised by wolves
Is eventually only able to growl
I growl for people to go away
While my tail wags for them to stay
I never was good at being a wolf
Though I caught the lust of solitude
My fur is too rough to be indoors
But my paws are too soft for the streets
So I limp along, scavenging for food
Growling to cover my whimpers

Brother

February 2, 2020

Part 1

you were
my bully
my tormentor

I needed
a friend
a partner

But the abuse drove you to my throat
instead of to my aid

We should have been
a team
a pair

instead you destroyed me

there can be no rivalry
when all the pain
comes from one side

Part 2

When asked how many siblings I have
I don't know how to answer
They left together but
I left alone
All alone

Grown men cannot be
brothers
If brothers are only
bullies
and I told myself
I would get away from that life
forever

Anchors – Away

February 3, 2020

Part 1

If you never get a boat
You never need an anchor
You float and drift about
With nothing
Dragging you down or
Mooring you to the shore
Without an anchor there is no
Captain to shout orders or
Crew to keep happy and fed
Without an anchor there is no
ship
But at least there's freedom
Right?

Part 2

They say:
"people want what they can't have"
"comparison is the thief of joy"
"other people have it worse"
"be grateful for what you've got"

It's easy for those with full bellies to tell
a hungry mouth to stay closed
It's easy for those on shore to call for the
drowning swimmer to keep treading water

What isn't easy is to make
a lifetime supply of muck
fit into your tiny dirty bucket

What isn't easy is to hold
a stack of hot coals
without crying out

What isn't easy is to live
in a hurricane and not
let yourself get blown away

If you aren't there
you don't decide what easy is
sounds easy enough
right?

Graveyard

February 4, 2020

Part 1

I keep your bones
Even though the flesh has rotted away
Your head balances on my tower of skulls
It reeks but at least it's honest

Unlike you
When you said you'd be there for me
Unlike you
When you said everything was okay
Unlike you
When you said I was worth the effort

You weren't the first
And you won't be the last
But I will study your skeleton
Looking for the fatal flaw
In mine

Part 2

I walk where they've been buried
When I come back into town
I feel the ghosts under my feet
I even see some in person
Some people mock what they don't understand
But not me – I mourn it
Hold funerals for my expectations
While I watch my friends
Step into their graves

Locks

February 5, 2020

Part One

Brick, wood, plaster
Screaming, cussing, pushing
Stacks of papers and books
Tear stained pages
Locks that don't hold
Carpets worn and stained

There is no "where the heart is"
When everyone around you is heartless

Part Two

I used to live out of my car
But never inside of it
When I lived in a house
I slept outside

My apartments have always been tiny
But at least when I live alone
I don't have to lock the doors

Mean Girls

February 6, 2020

Part 1

Petite and perfect
Cruel and cliché
Manicured and malicious

Venom drips from their porcelain throats
Eyes glare darker than volcanic ash
Polished lips utter sentences of death

They're called Mean Girls, or Bitches to be crass
Queens of all they trod on
Crushing the rest of us with their sparkling heels

They infested my school
They reigned at my church
One lurked in my house

Nowhere was safe
For an ordinary girl
Like me

Part 2

She traded her lipstick for Carmex to use in the Himalayas
Her mini skirts have morphed into yoga pants
She keeps her nails short instead of manicured

The Mean Girl in her might be dormant
But I still feel the burn of her hatred
In the back of my head every day

Pet Cemetery

February 7, 2020

Part 1

Gosling with a broken neck
Baby bird thrown from the railing
Angel has a limp and Roxy has a snarl
The cat is scared of other humans

When I got Sly I was worried that
I wouldn't know how to
Love an animal
Who hadn't been abused

Part 2

We buried the bunnies in the backyard
Friskel lies in Hidden Valley
I never saw my dogs again
But maybe it's better that way

We grew up together
All skittish, all scared
I raised my new cat to be strong
If only I could do the same for myself

Snow Day

February 8, 2020
The only snow of the year

Part 1

Wet gloves stretched thin against
the hot glass of the fireplace
Watching the news early praying that
Our schools would be among those closed
Wanting permission from neighbors for
the luxury of scraping snow off their cars

In Alabama, as in Tennessee,
snow days are few and revered
Holy angels, rolled snowmen,
catching flakes on our tongues
Rituals to try to be like other kids
Kids who have snow, kids who have fun
White covers our yard just like everyone else's
No one can see the filth that lies underneath

Part 2

I go far away looking for snow falling
Instead it falls outside my window
Sudden, unexpected, fleeting
Soft snow covers my lack of faith
I walk alone with no distractions
The day will go on, but I will stay
In the snow

Freedom

February 9, 2020

Part 1

I want to run away
Or get abducted by aliens
Or adopted into another family

I hide in a tree
In the closet
Under my bed

I can't stand the yelling
At me or at the others
It often comes with action

I get drug around
Where they want to go
I have to do
What they tell me to do
I cannot eat
When they tell me not to
I don't want to be
Who they want me to be

They control my situation
I can't control my emotions
So I become a pebble
Smooth but hard
I let them erode me
But I never let them
Take away my center

Part 2

I live alone
I walk alone
I travel alone
I heal alone

My sickness keeps me stuck
My emotions still are buried
Going some places alone
Is worse than not going at all

I managed to get away
But I was never good
At making connections
So now I'm floating
With a few tethers
But nothing solid
I'm held by hairs
Not by chains
I pull and they break
You pull and I break
Man wasn't meant to be alone
But I am no man
And I can't let anyone
Come in and break me
Again

Birthday Song

February 10, 2020
My thirtieth birthday

Part 1

It rained when I was born
Just like it's raining now
Storms have always been in my life
But so have refreshing showers
Where there's water there's life
Even though too much means death
I drown in my own abundance
Or suffocate in my perceived lack
Some people want to hide from aging
But I fought too hard to survive
To want to hide who I am

Part 2

Three decades of illness and abuse
I refuse to have three more
If I don't heal and learn love
I might as well stop having birthdays
Altogether

Church

February 11, 2020

Part 1

It was a place of danger
Even in the sanctuary
I learned cruelty
In the form of prayer
I hid from my family like
Adam and Eve hid from God
But when I was drug out
There were no garments of skin
To keep me warm

Part 2

Church shows sexism that pushes women into the dark ages
Christian radio spews hatred out like fire and brimstone
Bible studies reject, judge, and snub

Jesus respected women and took them as disciples
Jesus preached love as the most important commandment
Jesus showed compassion to those on the margins of society

I wonder if Jesus would have stepped foot inside our churches
And if he did
Would he turn over the tables or eat at them?

Sickness

February 12, 2020

Part 1

I was not allowed to lay down
To watch TV, skip my chores
Because I was too sick, too often

When my sister faked sick, she
received the luxuries of rest and recuperation
But not me – too sick, too often

I tried to vomit to prove my nausea,
To keep my eyes closed to prove my migraines
They made me too sick, too often

The school nurse said I was faking
My family said I was lying
How else would I be so sick, so often

That I'm still sick to this day?

Part 2

I've been called a liar my whole life
Parents, siblings, teachers
Friends, strangers, even some doctors
I wish I was lying

Instead I stay trapped
By sickness, exhaustion, lack
Desperately praying for relief
From what they don't believe is real

Lucky

February 13, 2020

Part 1

I remember when
People would call me lucky
When I worked hard
And call me skilled
When I was just lucky

It's hard to see myself as lucky
When so much has gone wrong
But I can't say I'm unlucky
When so much has gone right

Luck is like a drop of water
Pure but fragile
Ready to drop at any minute
And splash onto the sidewalk
Before it disappears

Part 2

I live in a whirlpool
It sucks in anyone who comes too close
Distorts them into
Funhouse versions of themselves
But the funhouse is from my nightmares
I watch my friends' faces distort and voices change
As they go from loving me
To wanting nothing to do with me
And I can't reach out
To pull myself into their world
So I have to push others out of mine
Before they get swallowed up

Valentines Monsters

February 14, 2020
Valentines Day

Part 1

When I was in middle school
I wrote a story about Valentines Monsters
But I had no idea
What monsters my Valentines would become
I thought love was fake
Later I wished it was
Maybe if love was fake
I wouldn't be so afraid of it now

Part 2

I spent eight years in relationships
Trying to burrow a home in someone else
I hoped to find a partner
But instead I found more hurt
I learned to be alone.

I spent nine years in solitude
Building up a fort so no one could hurt me
I stocked up on all I needed
But left everything outside
I wanted to need nothing.

I try to cultivate friendships
Begging people to come see me
I have given up on solitude
But still don't trust anyone
I don't know what's left.

Endings

February 15, 2020

All I wanted as a kid was to get away
I got rid of all my other dreams and ambitions
Only kept the goal of getting out

Getting everything you want is a lot easier
When you only want one thing
I got older but I didn't get happier

I could finally change my location
but I couldn't change myself to match

Part 2

I've been kept in storage and now I'm in quarantine
I've lived out of a backpack and now I live stuck
I've been dragged under the ocean so many times
I no longer know which way is up
Or how I would ever get there

So much has gone wrong
It's a miracle I'm still here
Or it's a curse

It's like in dreams when your feet are melting into the ground
And you try to scream but nothing comes out
And you're moving your arms slow and heavy
But in the end you get sucked under
By what nightmares are made of

www.ingramcontent.com/pod-product-compliance
Lightning Source LLC
Chambersburg PA
CBHW070958120626
46546CB00004B/1685